VIDEO BOOK

DRUMSET
CONCEPTS & CREATIVITY
Find Your Unique Voice on the Drumset

T0088356

BY CARTER MCLEAN

To access video, visit:
www.halleonard.com/mylibrary

"Enter Code"
4652-9232-2849-2458

Transcribed by Mike Dawson

ISBN 978-1-5400-3975-0

HAL•LEONARD®

Visit Hal Leonard Online at
www.halleonard.com

Contact us:
Hal Leonard
7777 West Bluemound Road
Milwaukee, WI 53213
Email: info@halleonard.com

In Europe, contact:
Hal Leonard Europe Limited
42 Wigmore Street
Marylebone, London, W1U 2RN
Email: info@halleonardeurope.com

In Australia, contact:
Hal Leonard Australia Pty. Ltd.
4 Lentara Court
Cheltenham, Victoria, 3192 Australia
Email: info@halleonard.com.au

CONTENTS

5   TECHNIQUE

5   PRACTICE

6   GROOVE CONSTRUCTION

7   PHRASING

7   TUNING

8   THE KALEIDOSCOPE & MORE

   9   Diagrams

   9   Kaleidoscope

   46   Groove Examples

   50   Single-Hand Exercise

54   GEAR

55   ABOUT THE AUTHOR

ABOUT THE VIDEO

To download or stream the video lesssons that accompany this book, simply visit **www.halleonard.com/mylibrary** and enter the code found on page 1.

TECHNIQUE

With technique comes a lot of responsibility. I understand technique as a tool that's used to communicate with other musicians. Technique doesn't dictate the music; it *serves* it. Just because you might have a blazing single stroke roll does not mean you ever have to use it. A lot of students want to get better hands and have more facility on the drums, but they don't know what do with this facility. If I could magically give you all the technique in the world, it would not necessarily make you a better drummer. Instead, what I want is for you to get to the point of having enough facility on the drums to express musically whatever is in your head. That for me is the only reason to have technique.

If you want technique to simply impress other drummers, I think your path could be, in the long run, very short. The music should tell you what technique tools to pull out in each moment. I want you to have every tool available so you can make the statements you want on the drums as the moment dictates. All of the exercises in this book are simple but can be applied in complex ways if you explore them thoughtfully. Technique is also about what you *don't play* and understanding the concept of space. I encourage you to explore that void: in music, purposefully choosing to *not* play something can be beautifully impactful.

PRACTICE

Practice: some get obsessed with it and some run away from it. I hope you fall in the middle some where—in a place that keeps you excited, interested in the drums, and, more importantly, creating music with others. I look at practice as a constantly moving target. Every day I wake up and try to come at my craft with a different focus, a fresh perspective, and an open mind.

If you get behind the drumset for just a short time each day with small goals, you will quickly achieve those goals. This, in turn, will give you a sense of momentum and accomplishment, which is a great feeling. When I was a kid, drumming was an escape, and I could work on it by myself anytime I felt like it. It was, and still is, a real anchor in my life. Practicing can be an anchor that centers you, providing structure and a sense of control in a chaotic world.

Let's turn now to specifics. There are some basic tools in your technique toolbox that you need to keep sharp. I still practice single stroke rolls, double stroke rolls, and timekeeping every day. Yes, these are basic rudiments, but they are also the inescapable foundations of drumming—corner-stones of technique that you can turn to no matter how difficult a certain phrase may be. If you practice these basics, you will never be caught off guard. Another basic tool is your sense of play. If you have a practice session where you get inspired and want to go on for hours, do it and enjoy it! As you get older and life pulls you in different directions, moments of inspired practicing are rare and beautiful things.

If you are practicing an exercise like the Kaleidoscope (see page 6), chip away at it slowly. Make sure you are rock solid with every element of one section before you move on to the next. Be clear and honest with yourself. Maybe you could play a part a little cleaner or develop more independence with your feet. Take it as slowly as you need to and be patient. As French sculptor Auguste Rodin once said, "Patience is another form of action." Really listen to what you are playing, realize you're learning, and let yourself have fun!

GROOVE CONSTRUCTION

Our job as drummers is primarily to keep time for the band and make the music feel good. Developing good time is a matter of practicing with a metronome and, more importantly, playing with other good musicians. This takes thousands of hours, so don't be frustrated if, after a few years of playing, your time is not yet amazing. You have "time" to keep working on it. Having good time begins with listening, which is the most overlooked musical concept out there. Try to really hear the space between notes and be comfortable with those spaces. When you play to a click, try these three things:

- First, try to nail the snare and kick to the click so that its sound disappears.
- Second, try playing consistently on top or ahead of the beat.
- Lastly, try playing consistently behind the beat.

Playing around the beat in these different ways creates a kind of micro-tempo that gives you more control over the rhythmic feel of different musical styles. A slow blues might be better played a little behind the beat to give it a laid-back feel. A rock or Latin tune might benefit from a little on-top feel to drive the band and create a sense of forward energy. Playing with micro-tempo is not about changing the number of notes you play or a song's overall groove. Micro-tempo is your tweaking of exactly where that groove sits in time.

Groove construction is very personal. I think about it as a painter might, with a blank canvas and all the brushes and colors at the ready. Maybe I'll choose to paint in black and white, or maybe I'll throw every color I have at the canvas. What paint to use is a choice, and that choice should be deliberate and carefully considered. Something as simple as a little drag or press roll on the snare can dramatically alter a groove.

Dynamics play a huge role as well. Try thinking of your hi-hat, snare, and bass drum as three faders on a mixing board. Play a beat with everything matched at the same volume. Now pick a voice— say, the snare—and pull it way up in the mix. Now you have a soft kick and hi-hat with a loud snare. Experiment with changing the levels of your three faders until you have total dynamic control over your hands and feet. This will add considerable value to your drumming technique tool box.

Groove construction also benefits from simplicity. Never forget that a groove can be as simple as eighth notes on the hi-hat! I encourage you to simplify your grooves and explore their micro-timing and dynamics. It's amazing what you can reveal in a simple rock beat if you apply these concepts. In the same way, you can explore percussion and auxiliary sounds such as shakers, mallets, mutes, brushes, and jingle sticks. Picking up a shaker is a choice that can lead you down some cool, new sonic paths.

Each musician has their own musical fingerprint. If you ask 400 drummers to play the same simple beat, they will all have subtle and unique things happening in their sound. That is the beauty of music and also the beauty of being you: you have your own voice that is inescapably yours and one of a kind. I hope you keep exploring and developing your voice on this instrument.

Good luck on your sound-exploring.

PHRASING

Phrasing is one of the most valuable tools we have as drummers. While we don't play melodic and harmonic instruments, we use dynamics (from soft to loud) and tempo (from slow to fast) as our phrasing tools to express ourselves on the drumset. I often take inspiration from the phrasing of singers and other instrumentalists. I recommend listening to the greats, such as Marvin Gaye, Miles Davis, Donny Hathaway, Charlie Hunter, Bob Marley, John Coltrane, Frank Sinatra, Keith Jarrett, Prince, James Brown, Ry Cooder, Bill Frisell, Sam Cooke, and Tom Waits, among many others. All of these artists use space, pacing, and contrast in thoughtful, beautiful, and effective ways.

I also think of phrasing in terms of a conversation. Imagine you're having a casual chat with a good friend or a shouting match with someone on the street. These are two very different ways of talking, and just thinking about these different kinds of conversation can dramatically impact how you play. If I ask you to play a conversation with a friend on the drums, you might drum something quiet, calm, and spacious. If I ask you to play an argument on the drums, you might drum something sharp, loud, and possibly more rhythmically dense. As with a good conversation, there is a give and take in music: you listen first, and then, if you have something to contribute, you play. You never play before listening! As a challenge, try to imagine and then play different conversation styles on the drumset. Be creative and push the idea as far as you can. There are as many ways of drumming as there are ways of feeling. Knowing how to listen, when to play, and how to phrase are all parts of your musical vocabulary. The more you expand your vocabulary, the more you can express your ideas.

TUNING

It's interesting that we use the term "tune" to describe tensioning a drum head. Usually we aren't striving after a specific pitch; rather, we're just going for a particular sound. It could be a high-pitched crack with a lot of ring to it for a funk tune, or a super fat and low-pitched sloppy snare, perfect for a slow jam. I think about tuning or tensioning in terms of three pitch/tension zones: low, medium, and high. There are infinite variations among these three zones, but that can quickly get overwhelming to think about.

Instead, next time you have an hour to practice, I urge you to experiment and take chances with drum tuning. Choose a drum in your kit and explore all the different ways it can sound and how its heads interact with each other. For me, there are no rules for tuning, and the basics I cover in this book's accompanying video lesson are just a starting point. Your task is to try things out and experiment! For example, try detuning one lug completely or cranking all the lugs as tight as they go. Hear what happens when you are an explorer of sound.

Another factor that affects tuning is drum heads. The heads you choose play a larger role in a drum's sound than you might think. I have played amazing-sounding vintage snares that had 50-year old heads on them. But when I changed the head out for a new one, the magic was totally lost. On the flip side of that, modern heads are so well-made that you can bring a cheap drum to life if you tune it well. Do some research to find your sound and what you like in terms of different head combinations. Each head also has a specific feel. I typically like single-ply, coated Ambassador heads, which to me feel the most alive and responsive. I find that a two-ply or thicker head does not have as much rebound or resonance.

A final factor to consider is drum muffling. Muffling is a way to augment a drum's sound, and there is no "right" way to do it. You can muffle a drum with a tea towel or a Big Fat Snare Drum mute. Muffling is also a very effective way to make quick sound changes in a live setting. There are dozens of muffling options today, and I encourage you to explore as many as you can. Again, be a sound explorer. Happy Tensioning!

THE KALEIDOSCOPE & MORE

This exercise is like a multivitamin for your ear, hands, and concentration. I have been developing this idea over the last few years, and it has opened up my playing. I call it the "Kaleidoscope" because it starts as one thing and, over time, slowly morphs into more and more layers of complexity. To run through the Kaleidoscope from start to finish in one pass is a huge accomplishment, and I encourage you to strive for that! (Set high goals: even if you fall short, you will be a better player for trying.)

I recommend starting with one page at a time and getting comfortable with it. Slowly add each additional page until you are playing through everything without stopping. This process may take a few days, months, or even a few years. But keep at it! The key is to be consistent and mindful with your practice. Whether you have five minutes or five hours a day to practice, try to practice *every day*. You will be shocked at how fast your hands and mind adapt and learn from your consistency.

The Kaleidoscope is organized into several different sections, with each one progressing through the following routine:

- Hands only: No feet are involved.

- Hands with the hi-hat: The hat is played (with the foot) on each beat.

- Hands and the hi-hat with bass drum: The bass drum will play along with the accented notes.

- Hands, hat, and bass drum in a 4 over 3 rhythm: The bass drum accents every third note, regardless of which notes the hands are accenting.

For each routine, the exercises are numbered 1–8 based on which notes are accented. In other words, in exercise 1, every note is accented. In exercise 2, every other note is accented. In exercise 3, every third note is accented, and so on. Because this set of exercises is focused on rhythmic accuracy and not developing speed on the bass drum, the lower numbered bass drum exercises (such as 1 and 2), in which the bass drum would be playing straight 16th or eighth notes, are not included.

The first thing the Kaleidoscope exercise does is get your hands used to three different stickings for the same accent pattern. Getting used to accenting the second stroke of a double stroke takes time and effort. Once you get this under your hands, the next step is to incorporate the hi-hat foot. When you introduce this pulse against the hands, it provides a steady counterpoint. Whether your hands are playing 16th-note or triplet subdivisions, the hi-hat pulse layers against the hands. This is powerful training for your ears in that it allows you to hear new composite rhythms against one another, all within a cohesive rhythmic system. (It reminds me of the multiple gears ticking away at different rates in a classic watch.) When learning these patterns, try to relax and breathe. This will help you focus.

Once you add the bass drum accents and pulses against the hi-hat part, you will have four layers happening simultaneously. Putting all this together is like juggling. It takes a lot of concentration to make the groove flow and feel good, so enjoy the process and remember that it takes time to develop this level of hand/foot/mind coordination. Once you have your four limbs working together, you can even try singing the individual hi-hat and bass drum accents and pulses. Keep at it; I guarantee that little bits learned every day will eventually lead to your becoming a more adept and confident player.

Here are some sample diagrams that can help you to visualize and feel accents within different sticking patterns. Watch the accompanying video for a clear explanation.

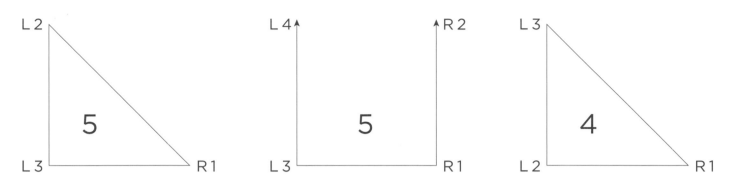

Singles Exercise - no feet

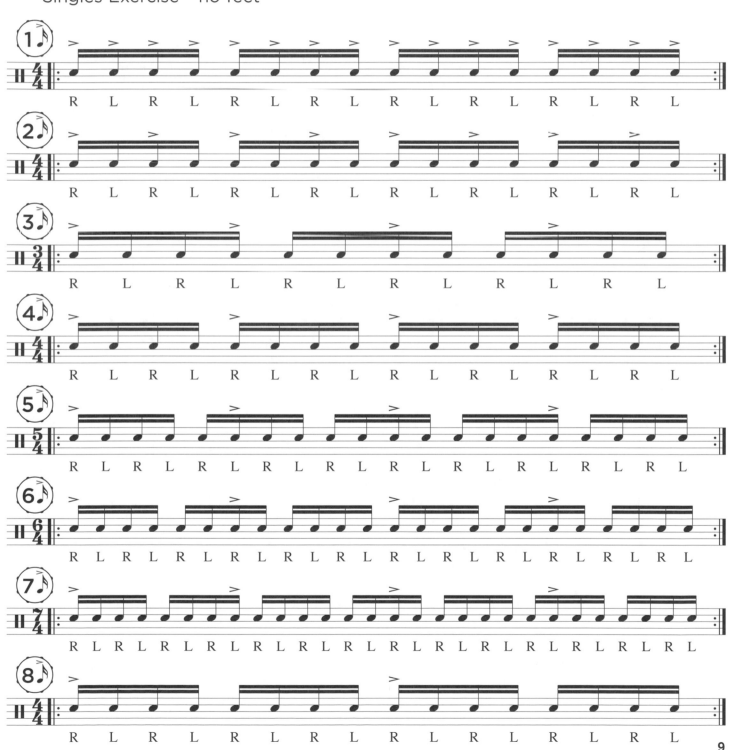

Singles Exercise - with hi-hat

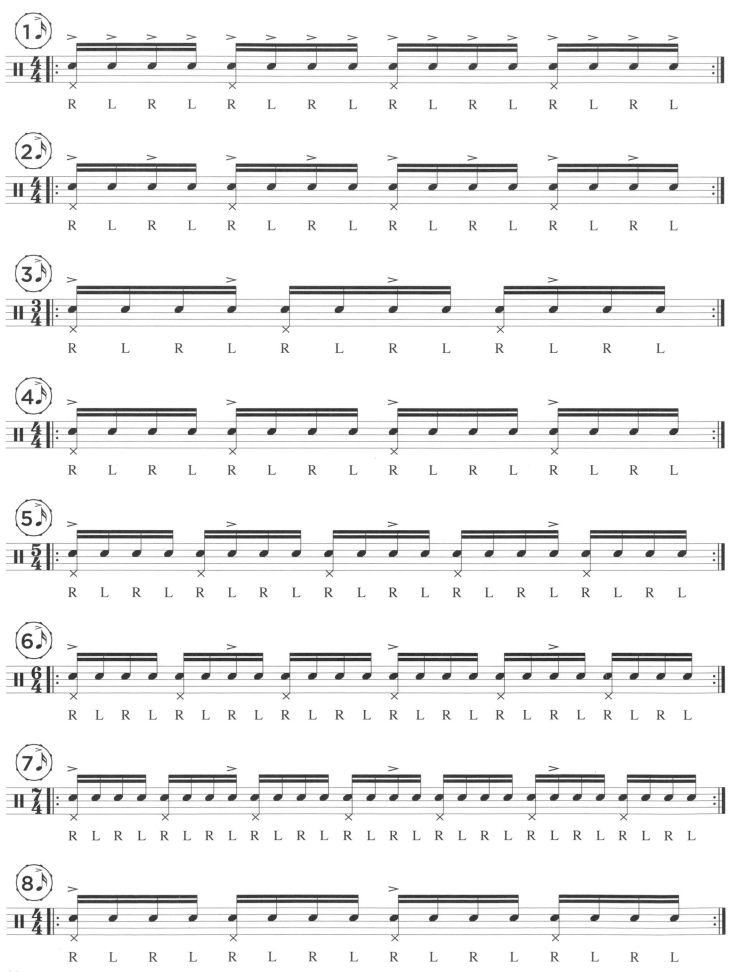

Singles Exercise - with hi-hat and bass drum

Singles 4-3, page 1

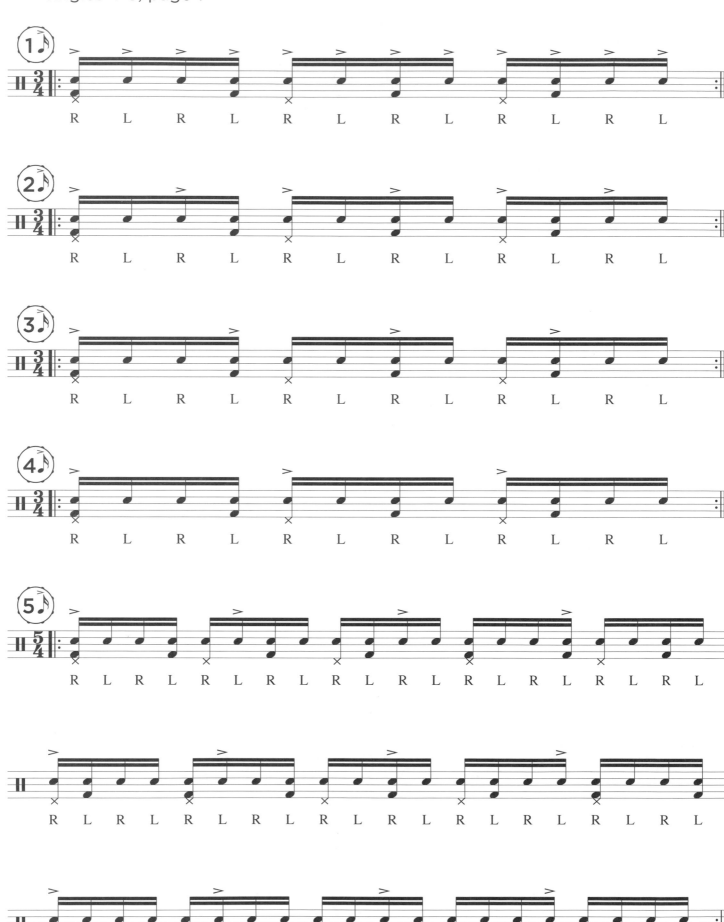

Singles 4-3, page 2

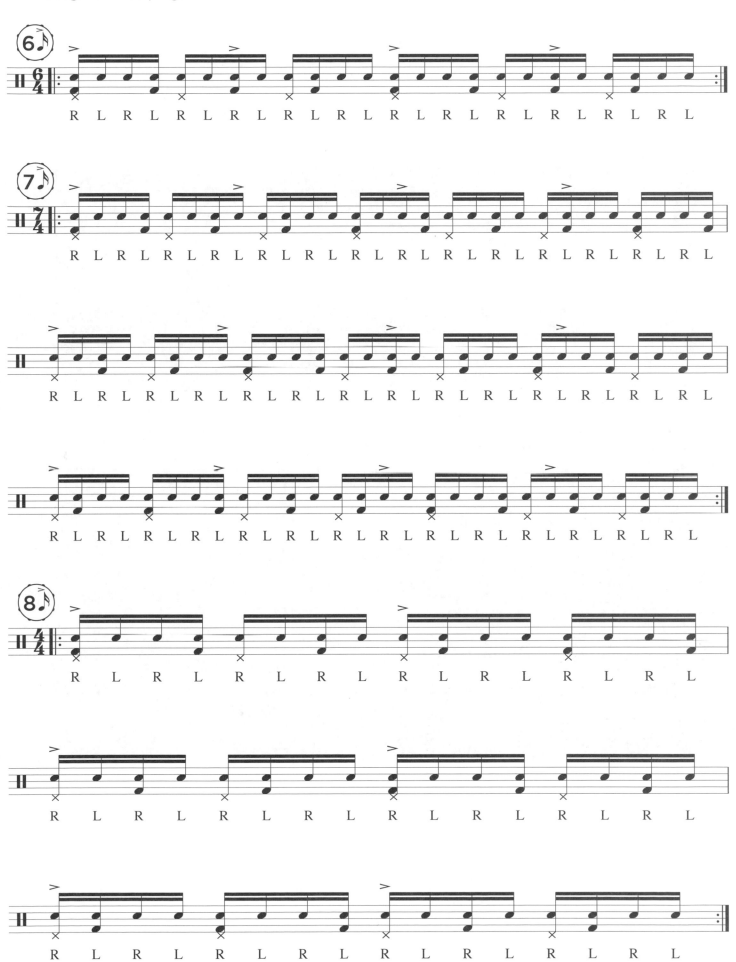

Doubles Exercise - no feet

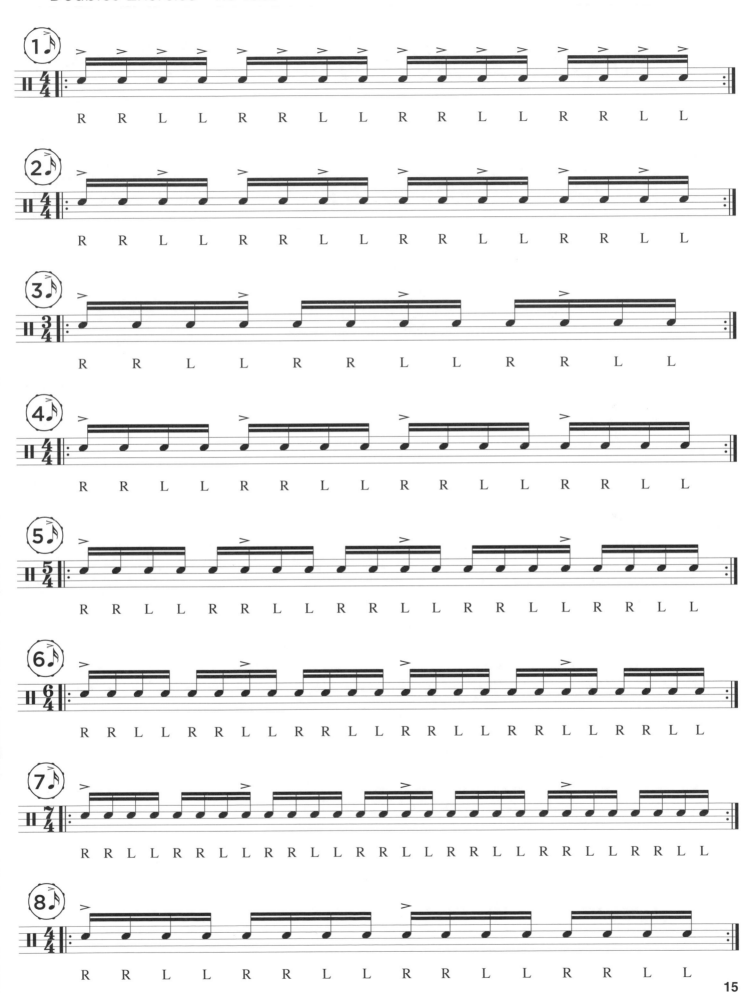

Doubles Exercise - with hi-hat

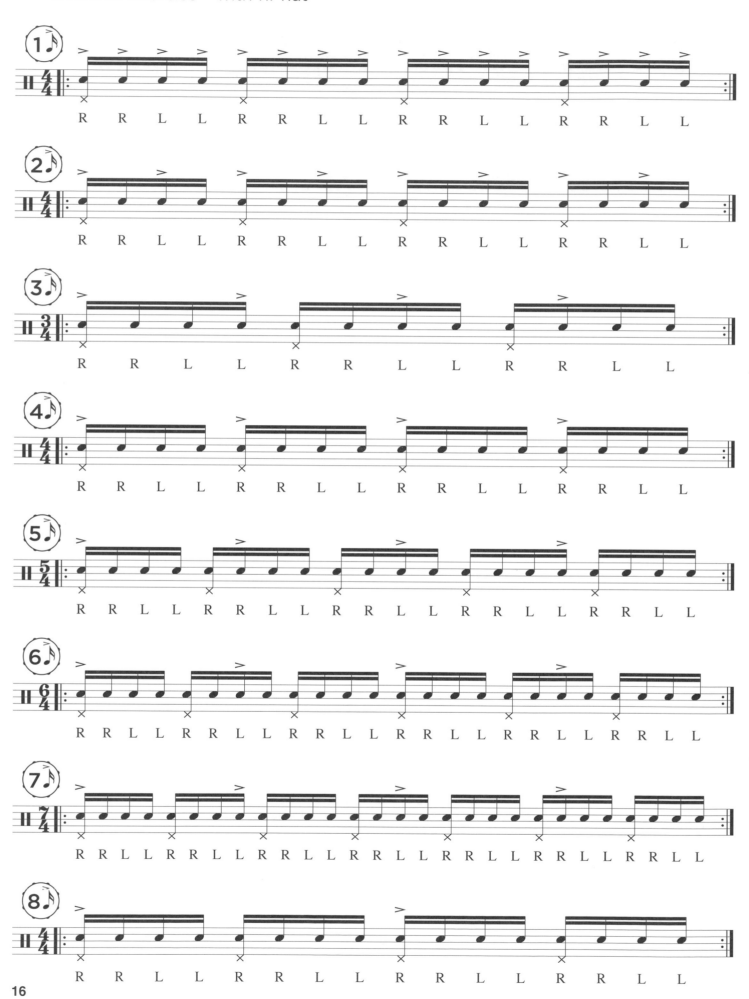

Doubles Exercise - with hi-hat and bass drum

Doubles 4-3, page 1

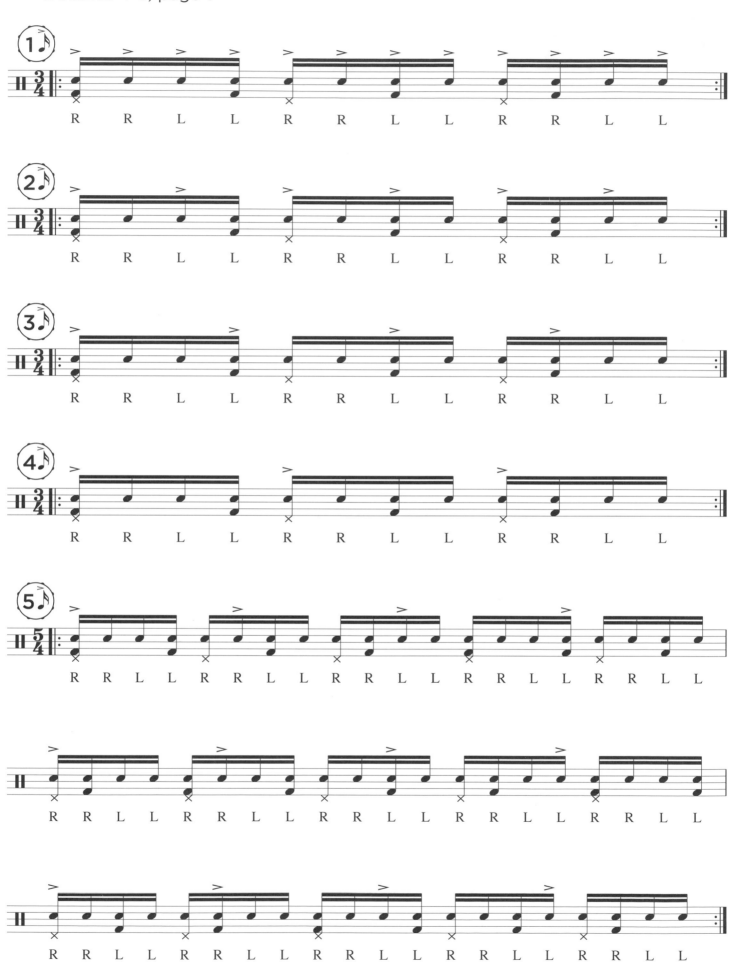

Doubles 4-3, page 2

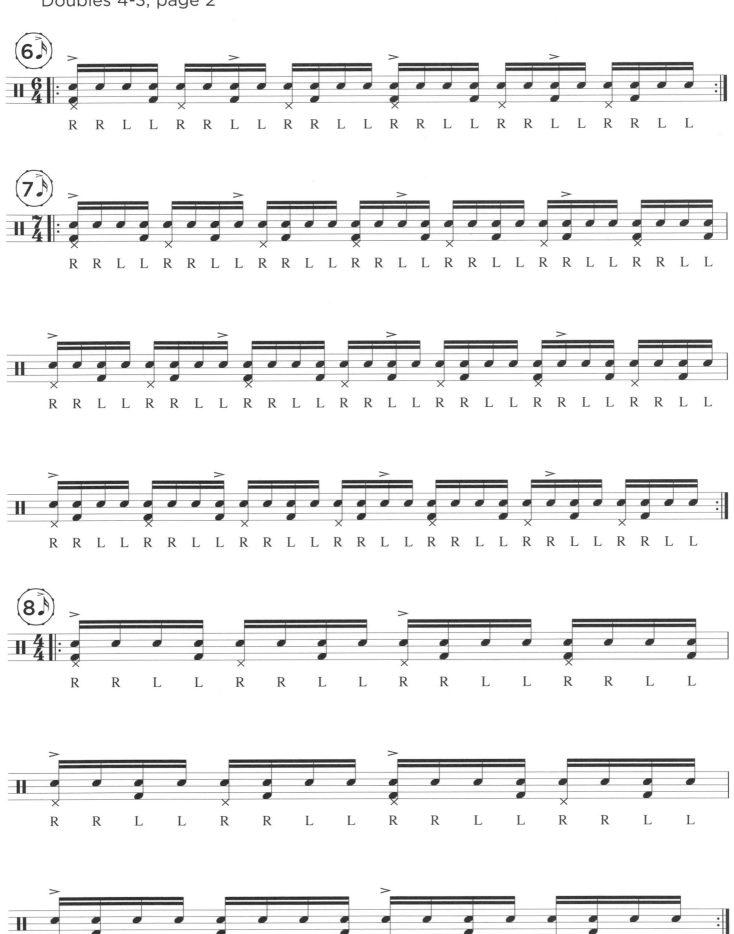

RLL Exercise - no feet, page 1

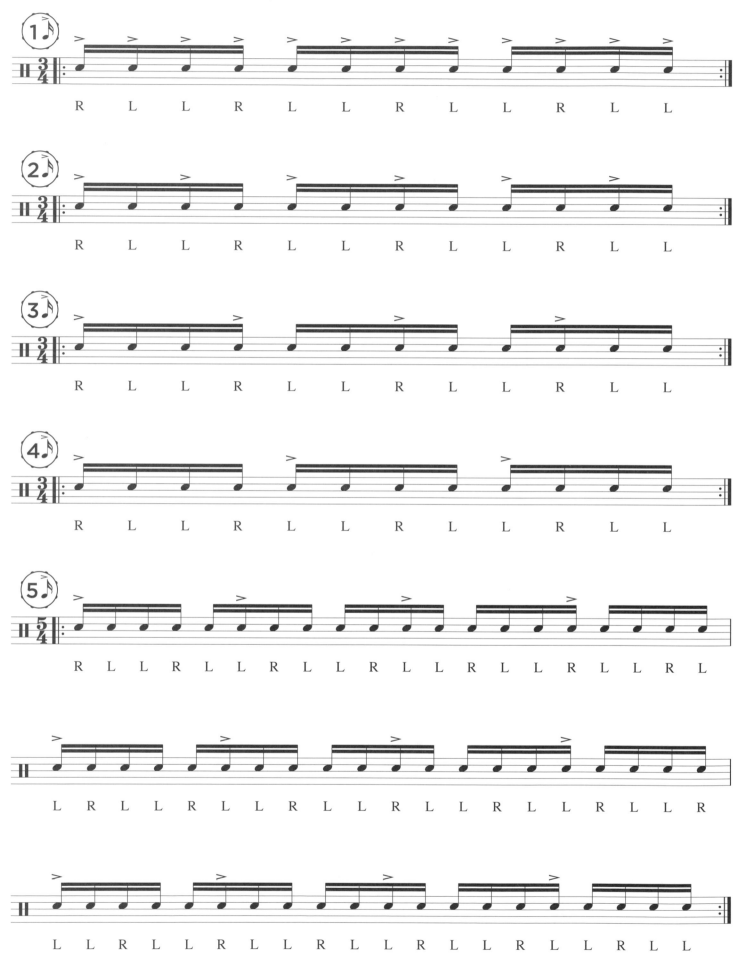

RLL Exercise - no feet, page 2

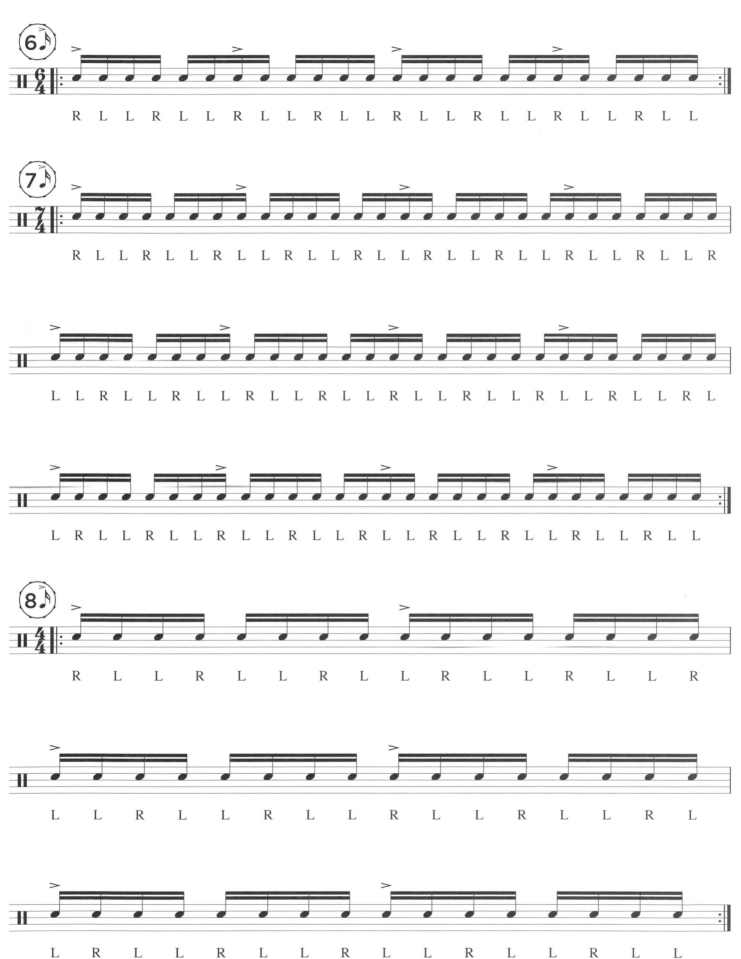

RLL Exercise - with hi-hat, page 1

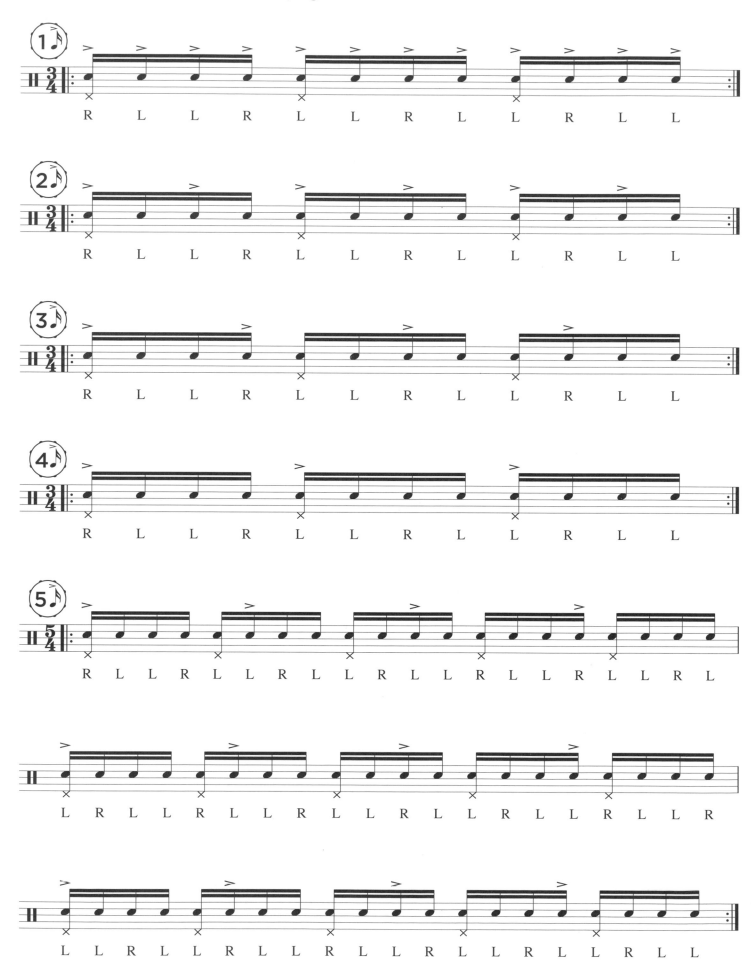

RLL Exercise - with hi-hat, page 2

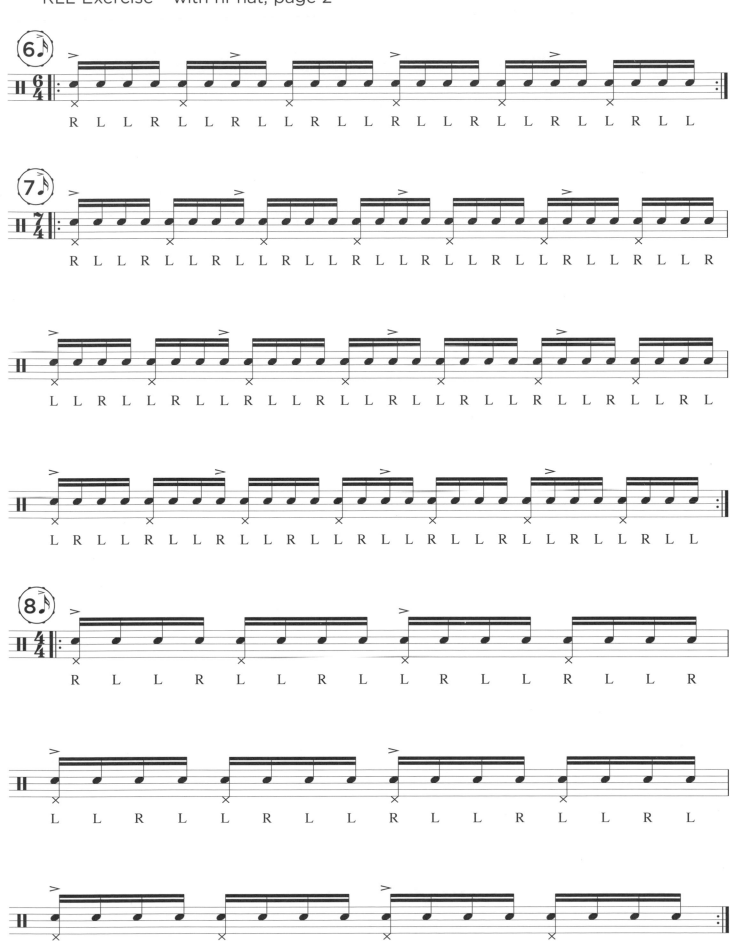

RLL Exercise - with hi-hat and bass drum, page 1

RLL Exercise - with hi-hat and bass drum, page 2

R L L R L L R L L R L L R L L R L L R L L R L L R L L R L L R L L R L L R L L R

L L R L L R L L R L L R L L R L L R L L R L L R L L R L L R L L R L L R L L R L

L R L L R L L R L L R L L R L L R L L R L L R L L R L L R L L R L L R L L R L L

R L L R L L R L L R L L R L L R L L R

L L R L L R L L R L L R L L R L L R L

L R L L R L L R L L R L L R L L R L L L

RLL 4-3, page 1

RLL 4-3, page 2

Triplet Singles - no feet

Triplet Singles - with hi-hat

Triplet Singles - with hi-hat and bass drum

Triplet Singles 3-2

Triplet Doubles - no feet, page 1

R R L L R R L L R R L L   R R L L R R L L R R L L

R R L L R R L L R R L L   R R L L R R L L R R L L

R R L L R R L L R R L L   R R L L R R L L R R L L

R R L L R R L L R R L L   R R L L R R L L R R L L

R R L L R R L L R R L L R R L   L R R L L R R L L R R L L R R

L L R R L L R R L L R R L L R   R L L R R L L R R L L R R L L

Triplet Doubles - no feet, page 2

R R L L R R L L R R L L   R R L L R R L L R R L L

R R L L R R L L R R L L R R L L R R L L R   R L L R R L L R R L L R R L L R R L L R R

L L R R L L R R L L R R L L R R L L R R L   L R R L L R R L L R R L L R R L L R R L L

R R L L R R L L R R L L   R R L L R R L L R R L L

Triplet Doubles - with hi-hat, page 1

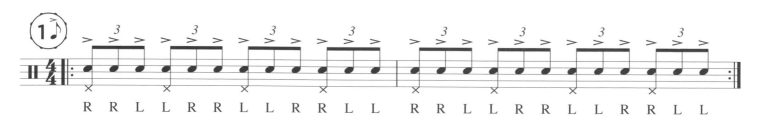

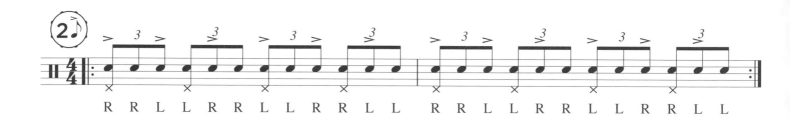

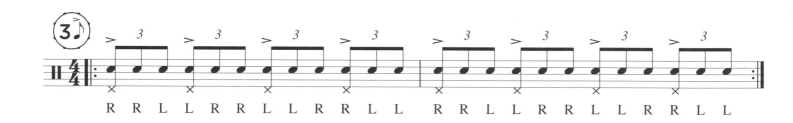

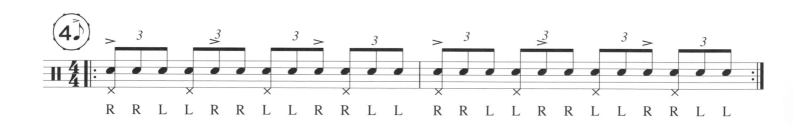

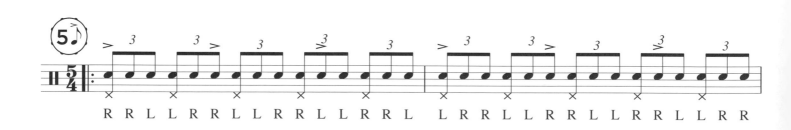

Triplet Doubles - with hi-hat, page 2

R R L L R R L L R R L L   R R L L R R L L R R L L

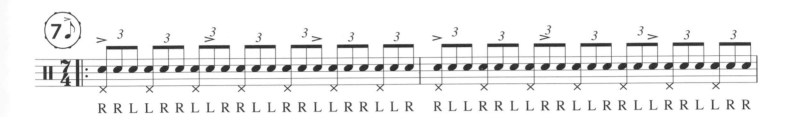

R R L L R R L L R R L L R R L L R   R L L R R L L R R L L R R L L R R

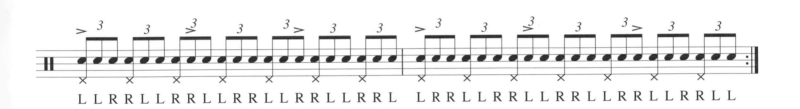

L L R R L L R R L L R R L L R R L L R R L   L R R L L R R L L R R L L R R L L R R L L

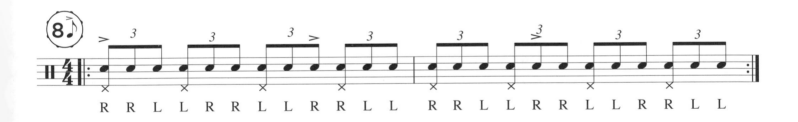

R R L L R R L L R R L L   R R L L R R L L R R L L

Triplet Doubles - with hi-hat and bass drum, page 1

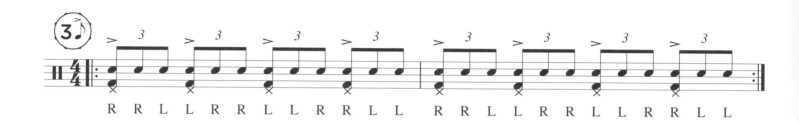

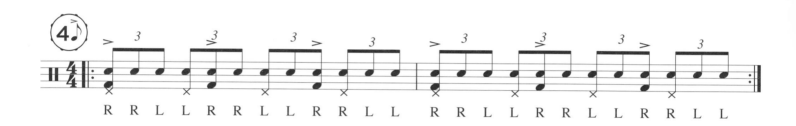

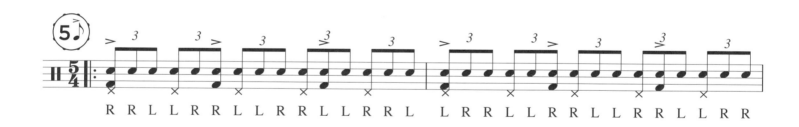

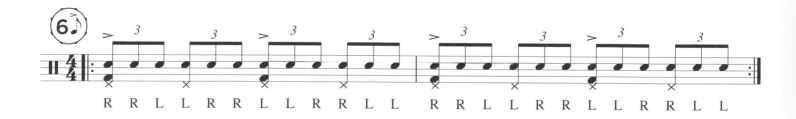

Triplet Doubles - with hi-hat and bass drum, page 2

R R L L R R L L R R L L R R L L R R L L R   R L L R R L L R R L L R R L L R R L L R R

L L R R L L R R L L R R L L R R L L R R L   L R R L L R R L L R R L L R R L L R R L L

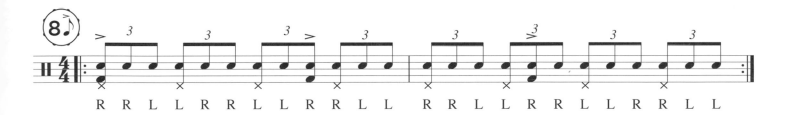

R R L L R R L L R R L L   R R L L R R L L R R L L

Triplet Doubles 3-2, page 1

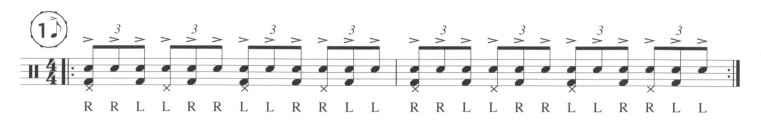

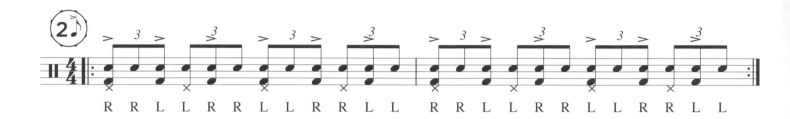

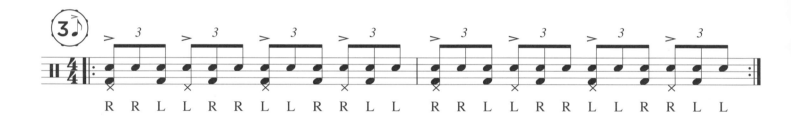

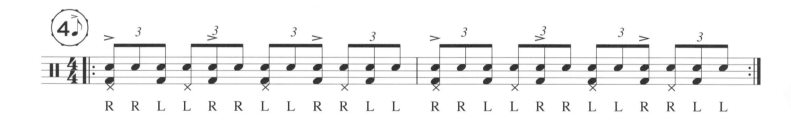

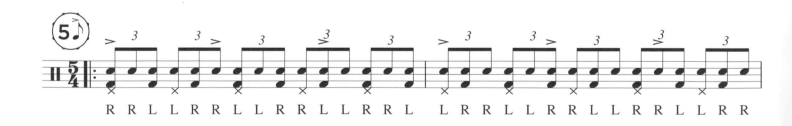

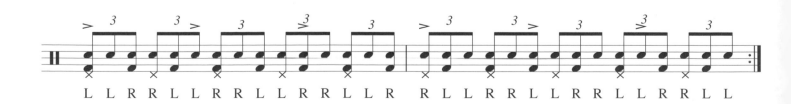

Triplet Doubles 3-2, page 2

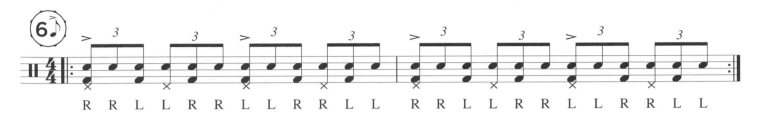

R R L L R R L L R R L L   R R L L R R L L R R L L

R R L L R R L L R R L L R R L L R R L L R   R L L R R L L R R L L R R L L R R L L R R

L L R R L L R R L L R R L L R R L L R R L   L R R L L R R L L R R L L R R L L R R L L

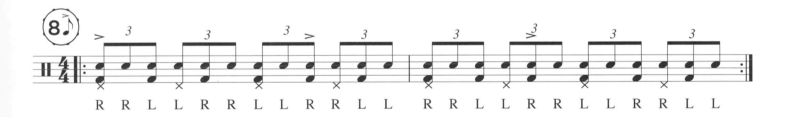

R R L L R R L L R R L L   R R L L R R L L R R L L

Triplet RLL - no feet

Triplet RLL - with hi-hat

Triplet RLL - with hi-hat and bass drum

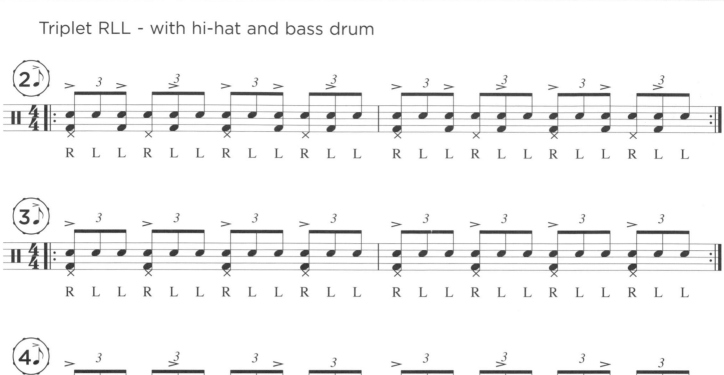

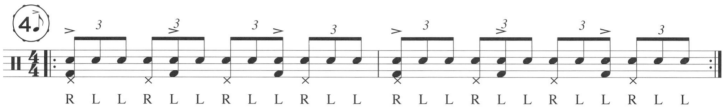

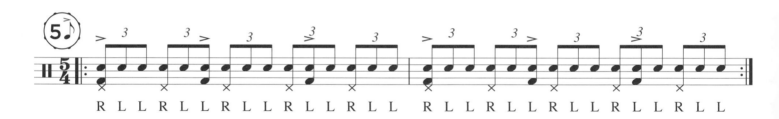

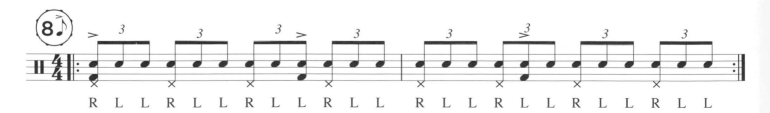

Triplet RLL 3-2

Final Exercise: 1-e-& Ride, page 1

Final Exercise: 1-e-& Ride, page 2

GROOVE EXAMPLES

Now try out the the following grooves.

16th-Note Groove

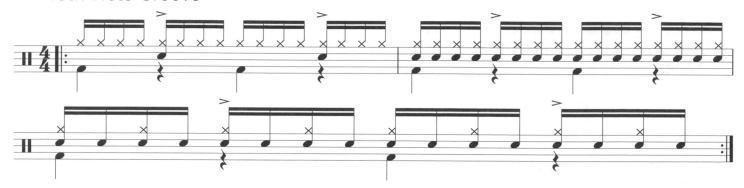

Doubles in 5's - with hi-hat and snare

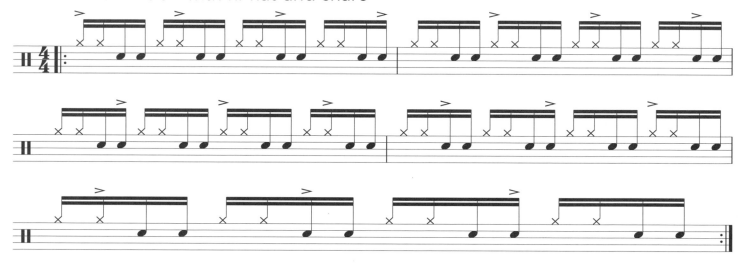

Polyrhythm Blues Groove

*Continue offbeat triplets with hi-hat foot.

RLL 4-3 Groove in 5's

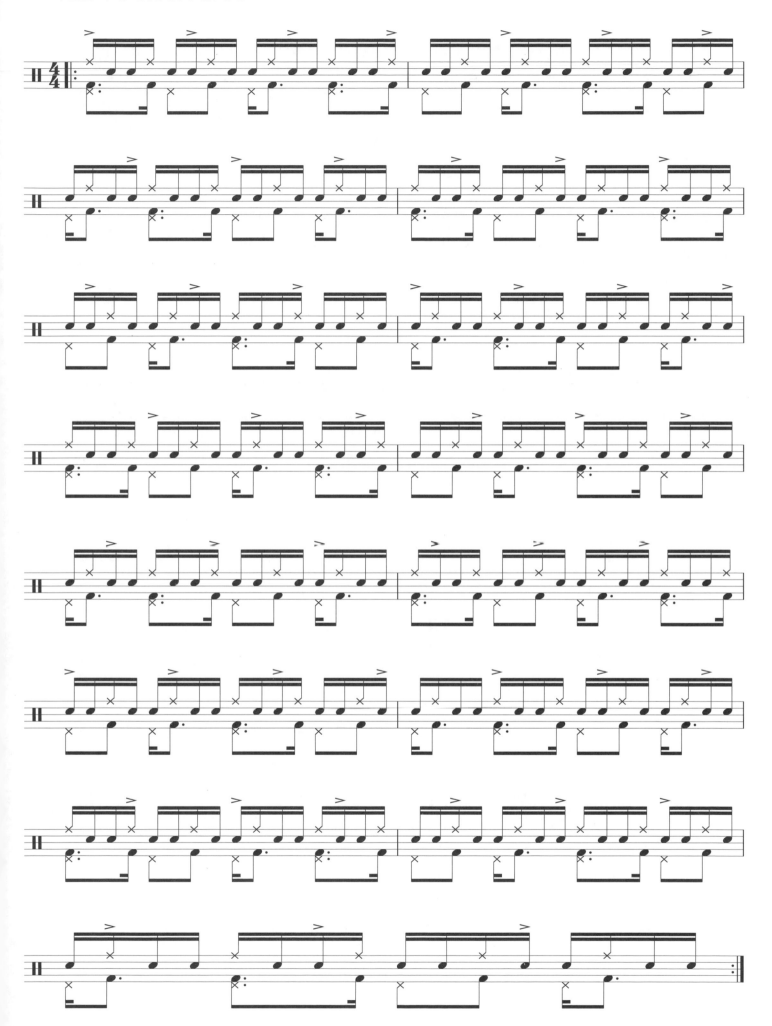

Crossover Grooves

R L R L R L R L R L R L R L R L

R L R L R L R L R L R L R L R L

R L L R L L R L L R L L R L L R L L R L L R L L

R L L R R L L R R L L R R L L R

R L L R R L L R R L L R R L L R

Modulated Shuffle - Basic, 3 Feels

One Kick, 3 Feels

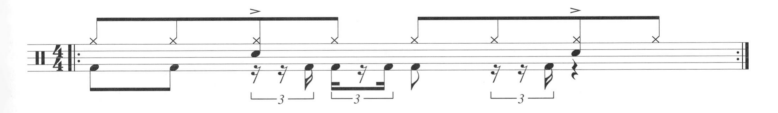

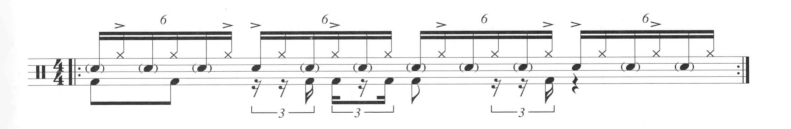

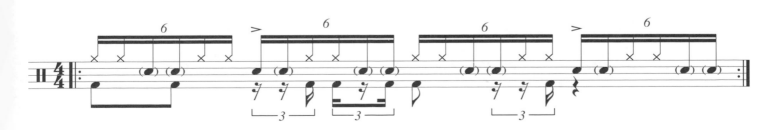

SINGLE-HAND EXERCISE

Here's a great exercise for working out each hand alone in 16ths. Check out the accompanying video for a demonstration.

Single-Hand Exercise - no feet

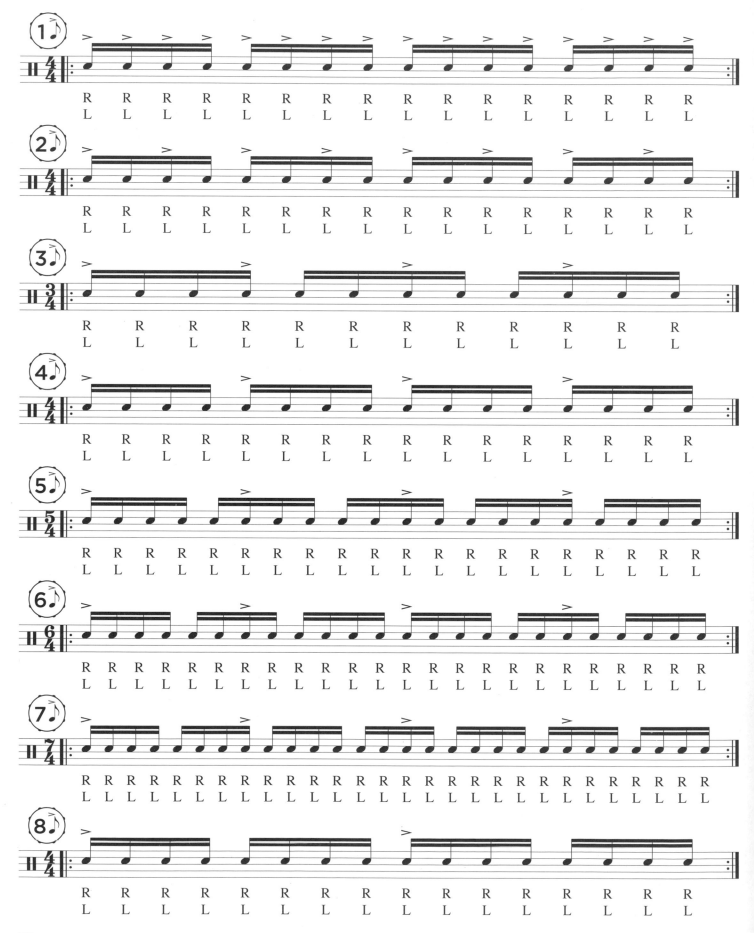

Single-Hand Exercise - with hi-hat

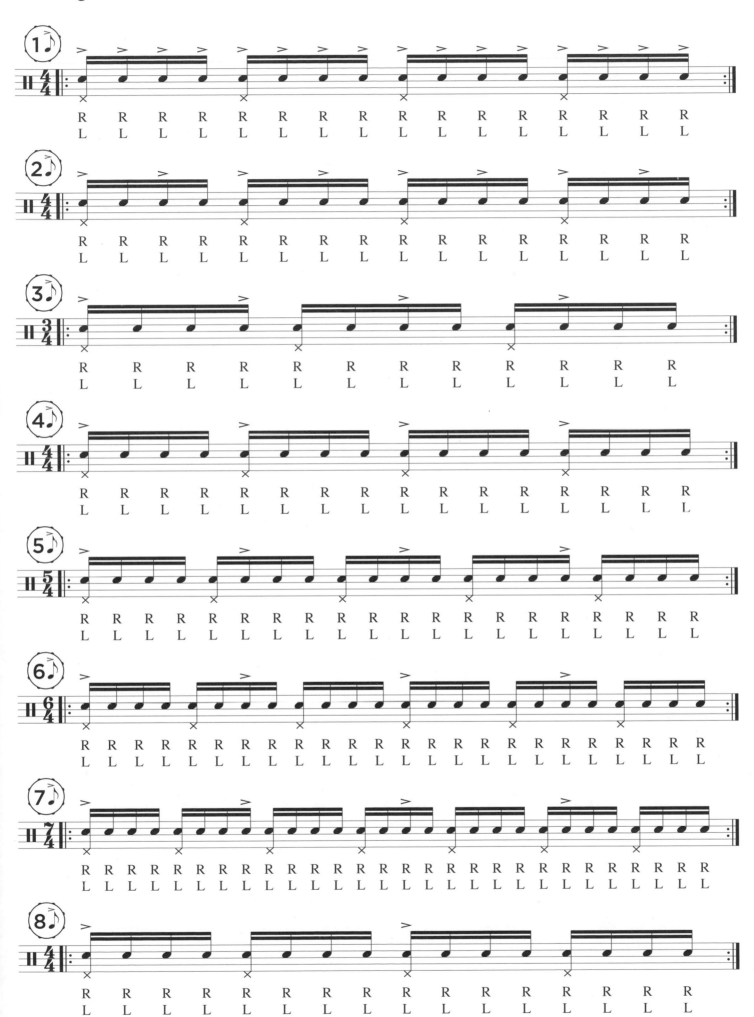

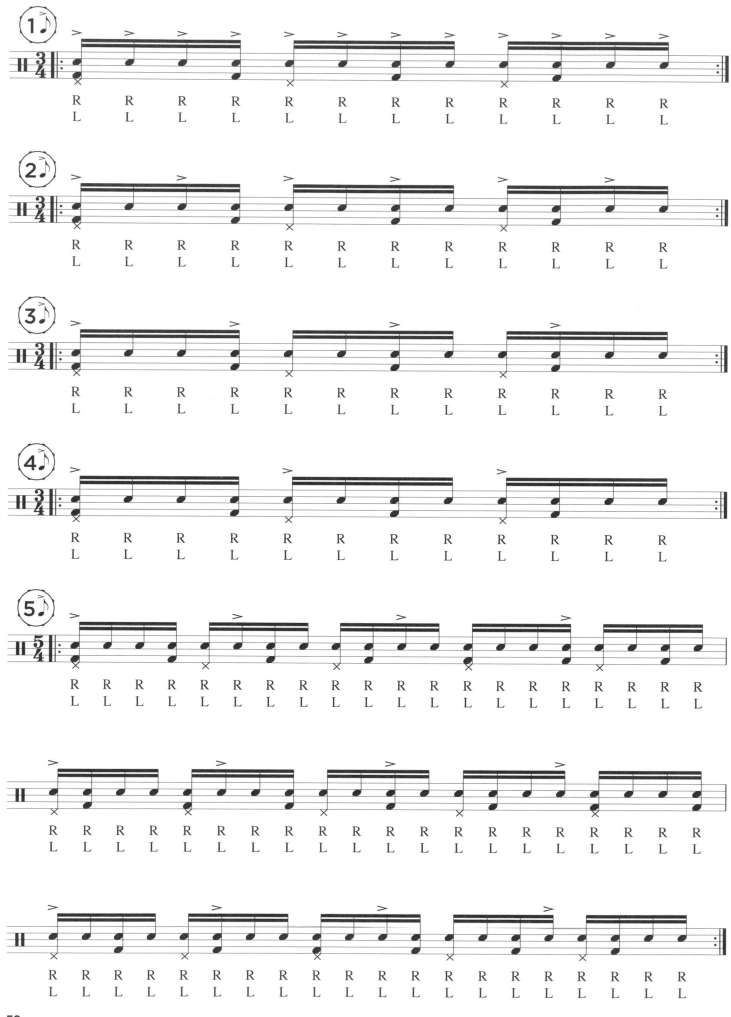

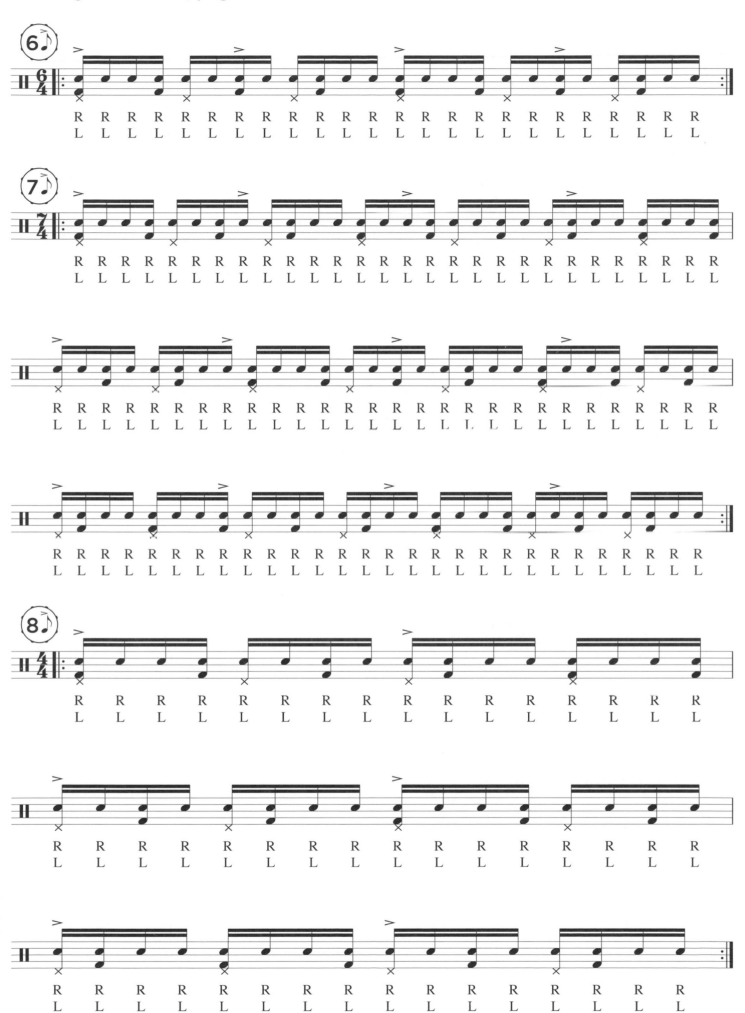

GEAR

DRUMS

Ludwig Legacy Maple Heritage, green finish: 8x12, 14x14, 14x16, 14x18, 14x20"
Snares: 5.5" Jazz Fest Reissue, 6.5" Copper Phonic, 6.5" Raw Brass,
various vintage Ludwig snares 1909–1970s

CYMBALS

Istanbul Agop 30th Anniversary
12, 15, and 16" hi-hats
20 and 22" rides
Signature 15" hi-hats
20 and 22" Chinas
20, 22, and 23" rides

HEADS

Remo Coated Ambassadors and Fiberskyn Diplomats
Controlled Sound Reverse Dots on snares

STICKS

Promark Carter McLean Signature sticks and various mallets, bundles, and brushes

HARDWARE

DW Ultralight

AUDIO

Earthworks microphones and preamps
Mics: SR25, SV33, DM20, and TC20
Preamp: 1024

Miscellaneous

64 Audio in-ear monitors
Universal Audio
Tackle Instruments
Demsticks
Big Fat Snare Drum
Morfbeats
Low Boy Beaters
Index Percussion
Thumb Thang Shaker

ABOUT THE AUTHOR

"Carter McLean is what sports writers call a 'multi-threat.' Along with playing some serious drums, he also plays tabla, guitar, bass, and piano. In addition, he's a composer, arranger, and synth programmer." —*Modern Drummer*

Carter was born in San Francisco and shortly thereafter moved to Connecticut. This is where McLean listened to and fell in love with music and especially the drums. At age 10, he started his journey as a musician. Broadway wasn't even on his radar when he started working at Manny's Music in Manhattan just prior to 9/11. The self-taught musician had just wrapped up his studies at University of Colorado – Boulder and was hoping to land a gig with someone like Sting, Peter Gabriel, or Paul Simon. But then, while working his shift and playing at the store, he got noticed by a vet of Stevie Wonder's band, Dennis Davis, and got invited to play with legendary musician Roy Ayers in Harlem. While touring with Melvin Sparks in 2002, McLean was approached to be a sub at *The Lion King* in NYC. This eventually led to McLean taking over the chair at the hit show in 2011.

From Charlie Hunter to the *Lion King* on Broadway, McLean has been busy touring, doing studio work, and maintaining a busy teaching schedule. In addition, McLean has shared the stage or recorded with Jamie McLean, Greg Holden, Charlie Hunter, Victor Wooten, Anthony Hamilton, Bernie Worrell (Parliament-Funkadelic), Fred Wesley (James Brown), Shelby Johnson (Prince), Melanie Gabriel (Peter Gabriel), Leni Stern, Matt Duke, and many others. Carter also released his own record *Ghost Bridge* in 2010, on which he sings and plays guitar.

YOU CAN'T BEAT OUR DRUM BOOKS!

Learn to Play the Drumset – Book 1
by Peter Magadini
This unique method starts students out on the entire drumset and teaches them the basics in the shortest amount of time. Book 1 covers basic 4- and 5-piece set-ups, grips and sticks, reading and improvisation, coordination of hands and feet, and features a variety of contemporary and basic rhythm patterns with exercise breakdowns for each.
06620030 Book/CD Pack.. $14.99

Creative Timekeeping for the Contemporary Jazz Drummer
by Rick Mattingly
Combining a variety of jazz ride cymbal patterns with coordination and reading exercises, *Creative Timekeeping* develops true independence: the ability to play any rhythm on the ride cymbal while playing any rhythm on the snare and bass drums. It provides a variety of jazz ride cymbal patterns as well as coordination and reading exercises that can be played along with them. Five chapters: Ride Cymbal Patterns; Coordination Patterns and Reading; Combination Patterns and Reading; Applications; and Cymbal Reading.
06621764 .... $9.99

The Drumset Musician – 2nd Edition
by Rod Morgenstein and Rick Mattingly
Containing hundreds of practical, usable beats and fills, The Drumset Musician teaches you how to apply a variety of patterns and grooves to the actual performance of songs. The accompanying online audio includes demos as well as 18 play-along tracks covering a wide range of rock, blues and pop styles, with detailed instructions on how to create exciting, solid drum parts.
00268369 Book/Online Audio $19.99

Drum Aerobics
by Andy Ziker
A 52-week, one-exercise-per-day workout program for developing, improving, and maintaining drum technique. Players of all levels – beginners to advanced – will increase their speed, coordination, dexterity and accuracy. The online audio contains all 365 workout licks, plus play-along grooves in styles including rock, blues, jazz, heavy metal, reggae, funk, calypso, bossa nova, march, mambo, New Orleans 2nd Line, and lots more!
06620137 Book/Online Audio $19.99

40 Intermediate Snare Drum Solos
For Concert Performance
by Ben Hans
This book provides the advancing percussionist with interesting solo material in all musical styles. It is designed as a lesson supplement, or as performance material for recitals and solo competitions. Includes: 40 intermediate snare drum solos presented in easy-to-read notation; a music glossary; Percussive Arts Society rudiment chart; suggested sticking, dynamics and articulation markings; and much more!
06620067 .... $8.99

Joe Porcaro's Drumset Method – Groovin' with Rudiments
Patterns Applied to Rock, Jazz & Latin Drumset
by Joe Porcaro
Master teacher Joe Porcaro presents rudiments at the drumset i this sensational new edition of *Groovin' with Rudiments*. Th book is chock full of exciting drum grooves, sticking patterns, fill polyrhythmic adaptations, odd meters, and fantastic solo ideas i jazz, rock, and Latin feels. The online audio features 99 audio cli examples in many styles to round out this true collection of super drumming material for every serious drumset performer.
06620129 Book/Online Audio $24.9

Show Drumming
The Essential Guide to Playing Drumset for Live Shows and Musicals
by Ed Shaughnessy and Clem DeRosa
Who better to teach you than "America's Premier Showdrummer himself, Mr. Ed Shaughnessy! Features: a step-by-step walk-throug of a simulated show; CD with music, comments & tips from E notated examples; practical tips; advice on instruments; a speci accessories section with photos; and more!
06620080 Book/CD Pack... $16.9

Instant Guide to Drum Grooves
The Essential Reference for the Working Drummer
by Maria Martinez
Become a more versatile drumset player! From traditional Dixielar to cutting-edge hip-hop, Instant Guide to Drum Grooves is a han source featuring 100 patterns that will prepare working drumme for the stylistic variety of modern gigs. The book includes essenti beats and grooves in such styles as: jazz, shuffle, country, roc funk, New Orleans, reggae, calypso, Brazilian and Latin.
06620056 Book/CD Pack... $10.9

The Complete Drumset Rudiments
by Peter Magadini
Use your imagination to incorporate these rudimental etudes in new patterns that you can apply to the drumset or tom toms you develop your hand technique with the Snare Drum Rudimen your hand and foot technique with the Drumset Rudiments a your polyrhythmic technique with the Polyrhythm Rudimen Adopt them all into your own creative expressions based on ide you come up with while practicing.
06620016 Book/CD Pack..$14.9

Drum Dictionary
An A-Z Guide to Tips, Techniques & Much More
by Ed Roscetti
Take your playing from ordinary to extraordinary in this a encompassing book/audio package for drummers. You receive valuable tips on performing, recording, the music busine instruments and equipment, beats, fills, soloing techniques, ca and maintenance, and more. Styles such as rock, jazz, hip-ho and Latin are represented through demonstrations of authen grooves and instruments appropriate for each genre.
00244646 Book/Online Audio ....$19.

Prices, contents, and availability subject to change without notice.

05
0